A RING-TAILED CAT ESCAPES DANGER BY CLIMBING A TREE.

Wonders of the
DESERT WORLD

by Judith E. Rinard

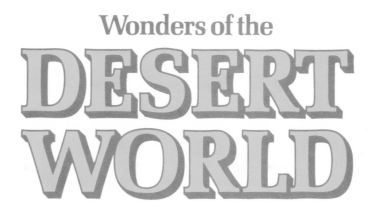

BOOKS FOR YOUNG EXPLORERS
NATIONAL GEOGRAPHIC SOCIETY

The moon rises over the desert. Soon it will be dark.
Cactus plants as tall as trees grow in this American desert.
A desert is a dry land where very little rain falls.
It is not easy to live in this land.
But many plants and animals do live here.

KANGAROO RAT

A rabbit rests in a shady spot.
During the day, the bright sun
can make the desert very hot.
The kangaroo rat also stays
out of the sun. It spends the day
underground and can live
without ever taking a drink of water.

COTTONTAIL RABBIT

GILA *(HEE-la)* MONSTER

A lizard called a Gila monster
crawls on the rocky ground.
The Gila monster is covered
with hard scales.
They look like shiny beads.
The scales help keep the lizard
from drying out in the hot sun.

Desert plants have many shapes.
A man looks up at a tall boojum tree.
It is shaped like a big carrot growing upside down.

A boy steps carefully among plants that grow on the ground.
This plant is called a caterpillar cactus. Do you see why?
Here, it grows beside taller cactus plants called chollas.
Most cactus plants have sharp spines but no leaves.
These desert plants store water in their stems and branches
and can live for months without rain.

CHOLLA (CHOY-ya) CACTUS   CATERPILLAR CACTUS OR CREEPING DEVIL

An organ-pipe cactus has many stems.
A snake climbs up a stem
to reach a bird's nest.
It is hunting for eggs and baby birds.
The mother bird screams at the snake.

BLACK RACER

ORGAN-PIPE CACTUS   SAGUARO (sa-WAH-ro) CACTUS

Many birds use the saguaro cactus.
Two woodpeckers have pecked
a home inside this cactus.
A tiny elf owl peeps out of
a hole in another saguaro.
The owl cannot peck out its home.
Instead, it finds an empty hole
and moves in. Another bird pokes
its head into a saguaro flower
and sips the sweet juice inside.

CACTUS WREN

ELF OWL

GILDED FLICKERS

CURVE-BILLED THRASHER

TEDDY-BEAR CHOLLA CACTUS

The cholla cactus has spines as sharp as needles.
If you touch one, it can stick you hard and HURT!
Yet this bird has its nest in a cholla.
The sharp spines protect the young from hungry animals.
A pack rat carries a piece of cholla in its mouth.
Then it finds a toy and picks it up, too.
Pack rats collect many things, and use them to build their homes.

CURVE-BILLED THRASHER

How do these animals keep from getting hurt
by the sharp cholla spines? Nobody is really sure.

SIDEWINDER RATTLESNAKE

In some places, the desert is very sandy.
The wind blows the sand
into small hills called dunes.
Animals that live here move easily in sand.
This snake moves by looping its body
sideways. So it is called a sidewinder.
The sand cricket has bristles on its legs.
The bristles help it move through the sand.
A beetle makes tiny tracks as it runs.
And a lizard with a long tail
digs into the sand and hides.

FRINGE-TOED LIZARD

SAND CRICKETS

PINACATE (PEE-na-KAH-tee) BEETLE

13

A mother coyote feeds her pups
in a shady den.
Outside, another coyote stands
on a rock and calls to its mate.
Two coyotes will often hunt for food together.
They hunt rabbits, mice,
and many other small animals.

Two coatis hunt for food in a desert tree.
They have come from their home in the mountains.
The coatis are looking for baby birds or eggs.
A coati has white spots around its eyes
and a white circle around its long snout.
Do you think these animals
look like they are wearing masks?
A coati also has long, sharp claws.
It uses its claws and pointed snout
to dig up roots and insects for food.

COATI *(ka-WAH-tee)*
OR COATIMUNDI *(ka-WAH-tee-MUN-dee)*

COLLARED PECCARY OR JAVELINA *(HAH-va-LEE-na)*

Peccaries, sometimes called wild pigs, live in the desert.
They go to a water hole to drink.
A mountain lion, or cougar, waits nearby.
The cougar sees a baby peccary and moves toward it.
But one of the big peccaries has seen the cougar.
The peccary snorts and chases after it.
This cougar gives up and goes away.

DESERT TORTOISE

CHUCKWALLA LIZARD

Desert animals protect
themselves in many ways.
A land turtle, or tortoise,
hides inside its shell.
A chuckwalla crawls between
two rocks. It puffs itself up
with air. Then it is so big
an animal cannot pull it out.

REGAL HORNED LIZARD

The horned lizard is
covered with sharp scales.
Not many animals try to eat it.
When the jackrabbit hears
the sound of danger,
it runs away.
With its long legs, it can
jump and run very, very fast.

ANTELOPE JACKRABBIT

Three birds called roadrunners
watch a rattlesnake crawling on the ground.
Roadrunners use their sharp beaks to kill rattlesnakes.
But the birds leave this snake alone. Maybe it is too big.
Nearby, another rattlesnake stops at a water hole to drink.

DIAMONDBACK RATTLESNAKE

TARANTULA AND WASP (TARANTULA HAWK)

Baby scorpions ride on their mother's back.
Do you see the sharp stinger at the end of her tail?
A wasp fights a big tarantula and stings it.
Then the tarantula cannot move.
The wasp drags it to a hole and lays an egg on it.
When the egg hatches, the baby eats the tarantula.

For months
the desert has been dry.
But now, the sky is suddenly
filled with clouds.
Rain begins to fall.
The rain pours down hard.
Sometimes the water
rushes over the land
and makes muddy rivers.
Then, as suddenly as it began,
the rain stops.
The sun shines again.
In some places,
the red mud of the desert
begins to crack
as it bakes in the hot sun.
Soon, the desert
will be dry again.

Rain brings life to the desert.
Tiny tadpoles suddenly appear in pools
made by the rain. How do you think
these tadpoles got there?
When it rained, the mother toad
came up out of the ground.
She mated with a male toad
in a rainpool and laid her eggs there.
The tadpoles hatched from these eggs.
The rainpool will dry up in a short time.
But these tadpoles grow so fast
that they become toads
before the pool dries up.

SPADEFOOT TOAD

Diving beetles and desert shrimp also hatch
from eggs and grow quickly in the rainpools.

LARVA OF DIVING BEETLE

ADULT DIVING BEETLE

ADULT TADPOLE SHRIMP

Rain makes plants grow and flowers bloom.
The flowers fill the desert with bright colors.
Many of the desert flowers will not last long.
Some plants will grow sweet fruit.
In this land, there are many wonders.
The desert is full of surprises.

HEDGEHOG CACTUS FLOWER

YOUNG FRUIT OF CARDON CACTUS

PALOVERDE (PAH-lo-VER-dee) TREE IN BLOOM

BARREL CACTUS IN FLOWER

PRICKLY PEAR BLOSSOMS

Published by The National Geographic Society
Robert E. Doyle, *President;* Melvin M. Payne, *Chairman of the Board;*
Gilbert M. Grosvenor, *Editor;* Melville Bell Grosvenor, *Editor-in-Chief*

Prepared by

The Special Publications Division
Robert L. Breeden, *Editor*
Donald J. Crump, *Associate Editor*
Philip B. Silcott, *Senior Editor*
Cynthia Russ Ramsay, *Managing Editor*
Elizabeth W. Fisher, *Research*
Wendy G. Rogers, *Communications Research Assistant*

Illustrations

David R. Bridge, *Picture Editor*
Joseph A. Taney, *Design*
Suez Kehl, *Design Assistant*
Drayton Hawkins, *Design and Layout Assistant*

Production and Printing

Robert W. Messer, *Production Manager*
George V. White, *Assistant Production Manager*
Raja D. Murshed, June L. Graham, Christine A. Roberts, *Production Assistants*
John R. Metcalfe, *Engraving and Printing*
Jane H. Buxton, Stephanie S. Cooke, Mary C. Humphreys, Suzanne J. Jacobson,
Marilyn L. Wilbur, Linda M. Yee, *Staff Assistants*

Consultants

The staff of the Arizona-Sonora Desert Museum, Tucson, Arizona, and Mervin W. Larson, *Scientific Consultants*
Dr. Glenn O. Blough, Peter L. Munroe, *Educational Consultants*
Edith K. Chasnov, *Reading Consultant*

Illustrations Credits

Jen and Des Bartlett (1, 9 bottom left and bottom right, 11 top, 13 top, 17 right, 19 top, 23 bottom, 31 top left, top right, and center left); Jen and Des Bartlett, *Bruce Coleman Inc.* (9 top right, 18, 19 bottom, 21 top); Josef Muench (2-3, 26 both, 27, 30, 31 bottom right); Kenneth W. Fink, *Bruce Coleman Inc.* (4-5); M. W. Larson (4 bottom, 5 bottom, 7, 8-9 top, 12 top, 12 bottom, 13 center left, bottom left, and bottom right, 21 bottom, 22-3, 25 top, 28 bottom left, 29 top, 31 bottom left); Walter Meayers Edwards, *National Geographic Staff* (6, 8 left, 14 top, 15, 16-17, 20 bottom); David Muench (10); George Olin (11 center and bottom); John S. Flannery, *Bruce Coleman Inc.* (14 bottom, 20 top); John A. L. Cooke, *Bruce Coleman Inc.* (24); Paul A. Zahl, *National Geographic Staff* (25 bottom); Robert F. Sisson, *National Geographic Natural Science Photographer* (28 bottom right, 29 bottom left and bottom right); M. P. L. Fogden, *Bruce Coleman Inc.* (32).

Cover Photograph: Jen and Des Bartlett, *Bruce Coleman Inc.*

A rattlesnake is coiled
on the desert sand.
It rests in the daytime.
But at night, when it is cool,
the snake hunts for food.

A black-footed ferret looks out of its underground home. There are very few of these animals left in the world.

Animals in Danger
Trying To Save Our Wildlife

☐ BOOKS FOR YOUNG EXPLORERS
☐ NATIONAL GEOGRAPHIC SOCIETY

In faraway Africa, a cheetah cub licks its mother's face.
Another little cheetah stretches after a nap.
Now it is ready to play. The mother swats the cub
with her strong front paw. It is a rough game, isn't it?
But it helps the cub grow strong and learn how to hunt.

Cheetahs are in danger because people have killed so many
of them for their skins. People are also using the land
the cheetahs need to hunt for their food.
Soon there may not be any wild cheetahs left. Other animals
are also in danger of disappearing from the earth forever.

A cheetah hunts alone.
It creeps forward slowly
and tries to sneak up close
without being seen.

Then it begins to run. Suddenly, it dashes forward
and runs faster than any other animal in the world.
This young cheetah catches an animal to eat.
Some animals hunt. Others are hunted. That is the way of the wild.

A woman wears a coat made of cheetah skins.
People have killed many cheetahs
to make coats like this one.
Laws to protect cheetahs
may help save these animals.

The wolf hunts for its food, too. Three gray wolves meet
on a snowy hill. They wag their tails and lick each other on the face.
Wolves live and hunt together in groups called packs.
How many wolves do you see in this large pack?
The leader lopes through the snow on a long hunt for food.

A farmer tries to shoot a wolf. He is afraid
the wolf will kill his farm animals.
People have killed so many wolves
that they have disappeared from many places.
Now laws protect some of the wolves that remain.

A wet baby bear huddles next to its mother.
Can you see why two older bear cubs are following their mother?
She has caught a fish for them to eat.
A young bear with a fish of its own plops into the river.

A park ranger moves
a bear to a place away from people.
Wild animals need to live
in a place of their own.

Two elephants push each other with their trunks.
They are trying to show how strong they are.
In contests like this, elephants almost never stab
each other with their tusks.
But when elephants fight,
they use their tusks to cut and slash.

11

Two hungry elephants snap twigs and rip leaves
from trees. Elephants need a lot of food.
Each day they eat leaves from many, many trees.

These mothers and calves go to a water hole to drink
and bathe. Elephants suck water up into their trunks
and give themselves showers.
A trunk can also scratch an itch or rub an eye.
It can lift a log or smell danger in the wind.

In Africa, a farmer grows food
on land where elephants once lived.
Soon there may not be enough wild land
for elephants to find food for themselves.

Zoom! A pelican dives into the water to catch a fish.
Do you see the fish the bird has caught?
It is in the pelican's pouch.
Soon the bird flies back to its nest.
There, a hungry young pelican pokes its head
deep inside the mother's pouch to get its food.

A man kills an insect with a poison spray.
If the spray goes into the water,
it may poison many of the fishes there.
When pelicans eat fish, they may be poisoned, too.
Now there are laws against using some insect poisons.

A bald eagle sits on a branch.
It is holding a fish in its sharp claws.
High above the water in a tall tree, young eaglets wait in a nest.
Their parents will bring them food
until they are old enough to leave the nest.
Then the little eagles can begin to feed themselves.

A man cuts down a tree
to make room for houses.
Eagles have lost another tree
where they could build nests.
In places called refuges,
people save trees for eagles.

The golden lion marmoset is a very small monkey.
This family of four marmosets lives in a zoo.
The father leans over to sniff one of his twin babies.
At the same time, the mother stretches out to rest.
Can you see the other baby? It is climbing on its mother's back.

A baby marmoset born in a zoo drinks from a bottle.
Scientists are raising marmosets and other rare animals in zoos.

A giant gorilla
munches
a leafy vine.
This great ape
lives in a
mountain forest
in Africa.
Sometimes gorillas
stand up tall
and thump
on their chests.
They beat
the ground
and hoot and growl.
But gorillas are
not fierce. They are
gentle and shy.

This gorilla baby
cuddles close
to its mother.
Another young ape
bends branches
to make a nest
for a nap.

Young gorillas
like to play.
They slide and
tumble and chase
and tickle
each other.

A scientist watches a gorilla.
Learning how gorillas live
may help us
protect these animals.

A herd of shaggy bison stampedes
across the grassland.
They sound like
the rumble of a thunderstorm.
Two male bison are charging each other.
They ram heads and bang horns.
They are in a contest to find out
which one is stronger.
They fight until one gives up. The loser
will turn away and begin to graze.

Bison, also called buffalo,
now live in protected places.
Once hunters killed so many of these animals
that there were only a few left.

24

A sea otter is resting
in a bed of seaweed called giant kelp.
The otter has wrapped the kelp
around its body.
This helps the otter stay in one place.
Then it lies on its back with its feet in the air.
This furry animal lives
most of its life in the ocean.

Sea otters dive deep underwater for their food.
Near the bottom, one otter has found
an animal called a sea cucumber.
The otter carries its food up to the surface before eating it.
Another otter holds a shellfish and scoops out the soft insides.

After it eats, the otter rolls over in the water
to wash away the food that sticks to its fur.

Men made laws against killing sea otters. People stopped hunting them for their fur. Now there are more otters in the sea.

Two humpback whales
swim slowly along.
They sing strange
songs underwater.
No one really knows
why humpbacks sing.
We need to know more
about whales
and other animals.
We also need to learn
how to share
the world
with whales and
all other living things.

People who care about whales are
trying to make other people care, too.
If people care enough,
they may save the whales
and many other animals in danger.

Published by The National Geographic Society
Robert E. Doyle, *President;* Melvin M. Payne, *Chairman of the Board*
Gilbert M. Grosvenor, *Editor;* Melville Bell Grosvenor, *Editor Emeritus*

Prepared by The Special Publications Division
Robert L. Breeden, *Editor;* Donald J. Crump, *Associate Editor*
Philip B. Silcott, *Senior Editor;* Cynthia Russ Ramsay, *Managing Editor*
Peggy D. Winston, *Writer*
Stephen J. Hubbard, *Researcher;* Jane Clarke, *Communications Research Assistant*
Illustrations
Geraldine Linder, *Picture Editor;* Jody Bolt, *Art Director*
Lisa Biganzoli, *Cartoon Artist*
Production and Printing
Robert W. Messer, *Production Manager*
George V. White, *Assistant Production Manager*
Raja D. Murshed, June L. Graham, Christine A. Roberts, David V. Showers, *Production Assistants*
Debra A. Antonini, Barbara Bricks, Jane H. Buxton, Rosamund Garner, Suzanne J. Jacobson,
Amy E. Metcalfe, Katheryn M. Slocum, Suzanne Venino, *Staff Assistants*
Consultants
Dr. Glenn O. Blough, Peter L. Munroe, *Educational Consultants*
Edith K. Chasnov, *Reading Consultant*
Ronald M. Nowak, Office of Endangered Species, U. S. Fish and Wildlife Service, *Scientific Consultant*
Illustrations Credits
Luther C. Goldman (1); Mohamed Amin, Bruce Coleman Inc. (2-3); Peter S. Thacher, Photo Researchers,
Inc. (3 top); Wolfgang & Candice Bayer (3 bottom); Dr. E. R. Degginger (4 top); M. Philip Kahl (4 center);
John Dominis, Time-Life Picture Agency (4-5 bottom); Thomas Nebbia (5); Tom McHugh, Photo
Researchers, Inc. (6 top); Gordon C. Haber (6-7 bottom); John L. Ebeling (7 right); Tom Myers (8, 22); Jeff
Foott (9 top, 16-17, 26-27); Mike Luque, Photo Researchers, Inc. (9 bottom); R. S. Virdee, Bruce Coleman
Inc. (10-11); Sven-Olof Lindblad, Photo Researchers, Inc. (12); Norman Myers, Bruce Coleman Inc. (12-
13); Michael E. Long, National Geographic Staff (14); Frederick Kent Truslow (15 top); Ralph W. Schreiber
(15 bottom); Jeff Foott, Bruce Coleman Inc. (16, 28-29 bottom); George Walters, Oklahoma City Zoo (18);
Frank Roberts, Animals Animals (19); Robert M. Campbell (20-21, 23); M. Woodbridge Williams, (24-25
top); Charles Palek, Tom Stack & Associates (24-25 bottom); James A. Mattison, Jr., M.D. (28-29 top, 29
center); Sylvia A. Earle, Sea Films Inc. (30-31); Fran Allan, Animals Animals (32); Cover Photograph:
Wolfgang Bayer; Endpaper Photograph: George Galicz, Photo Researchers, Inc.
Library of Congress CIP Data
Animals in danger.   National Geographic Society, Washington, D. C.   (Books for young explorers)
SUMMARY: Brief text and pictures describe the habits and behavior of a variety of endangered animals.
Cartoons explain some of the efforts being made to protect these animals.
1. Rare animals—Juvenile literature. 2. Wildlife conservation—Juvenile literature. [1. Rare animals.
2. Wildlife conservation] I. Title. II. Series.   QL83.N37   1978   599   77-95411   ISBN 0-87044-261-9

Cover Photograph: Mother Cheetah and Six Cubs
Endpaper Photograph: Bald Eagle

A pat from a mother's trunk
makes a baby elephant feel safe.